Also by Barbara Rose, PhD

Individual Power

If God Was like Man

Stop Being the String Along: A Relationship Guide to Being THE ONE

Know Yourself: A Woman's Guide to Wholeness, Radiance & Supreme Confidence

If God Hears Me, I Want an Answer!

Realigning Religion

Transforming the Unknown

Wisdom on the Other Side of Knowledge

The Messiah's Handbook

Being Enough NOW

Teen Relationships Adult Choices

The Ultimate Guide To Self Love

Get Over Him FAST

I'm Not in this Life to Please You!

Your Loved Ones Hear You: Explanations about Life on the Other Side

The Rush to Spend

Divine Intervention: The Cards Drawn from Your Soul

The Official Complete Guide to Higher Self Communication

BARBARA ROSE, Ph.D.

The Ultimate Guide to Self Love

R THE ROSE GROUP
Uplifting Humanity One Book at a Time ™

Barbara Rose, PhD

The Ultimate Guide to Self Love

The Rose Group
Uplifting Humanity One Book at a Time ™

Florida, United States
ISBN-10: 0979516153
ISBN-13: 978-0-9795161-5-3

You may contact the author through her Web site:
www.BornToInspire.com

Subject Classification
Health Mind & Body > Self Help > Self Esteem
Health Mind & Body > Self Help > Personal Transformation
Religion & Spirituality > Spirituality > Personal Transformation
Religion & Spirituality > Spirituality > Inspirational

Interior and cover layout by Toni Williams
www.livinginbloom.com

CONTENTS

CHAPTER 1

WHEN YOU DON'T FEEL GOOD ENOUGH

I f you have been feeling not good enough, how can you turn that around to authentically feel self love? I have asked myself this question throughout most of my life because for most of my life I did not love myself. I felt deeply insecure because I felt less than, not good enough. Perhaps you feel these same feelings. Perhaps, just as I used to, you feel like a failure, or somehow incomplete. Far too many people around the world experience the self-loathing that I used to experience, which is why I wrote this book. That experience must be turned around, and it can be turned around by you.

You see, when you believe all of the things you perceive to deem you as unworthy, all of those lies that tell you that you are not worthy in any area of your life, this breeds self-hate. I know this firsthand because I used to look at many areas of my life and feel deep dissatisfaction—areas such as relationships, finances, career, social status. And yet, it was not a relationship or career or finances or status that caused me to feel self-love. I learned how to love myself from writing thousands of letters to God, and I received answers. The result, self-love, led to this book.

There is no way for me to describe the sadness, emotional pain, heartache, frustration, and deep self-loathing that I used to feel.

I used to think that outside circumstances would make me feel better and happier. Perhaps you also think the same thing.

Perhaps you believe that a love relationship or a certain bank account balance will cause you to feel self-love.

There are many examples of people who do not love themselves despite their relationships and financial wealth. I am sure you can think of many people, perhaps even people you know, who truly do not feel self-love. It's one thing to say, "Love yourself." It's quite another to know how to do this. How can you feel self-love when you feel deep self-hate? Perhaps you feel deep depression. Perhaps you compare yourself to other people, just as I used to. As a result of those comparisons, we usually fall deeper into the not-good-enough category. At least I used to. So let us now take the view that your life and your feelings about yourself are pretty much at rock bottom.

Okay, this is admitting how you feel, honestly. Many years ago, when I told someone that I felt as if I was sitting in mud, that person answered, "Many people pay a lot of money to sit in mud." I instantly realized that this was, in fact, true. Many people go to luxury spas to have mud-bath treatments for beautiful, glowing skin. Those treatments are expensive, and people do pay a lot of money to sit in mud.

What if I told you that all of the feelings you currently have are a fantastic starting point in your life. Would you believe me? It is true. Admitting all of your true feelings now, acknowledging those feelings that cause sadness, is a great first step toward self-love. But it goes deeper than that because our feelings are caused by our thoughts and what our minds are focusing on. So rather than drag you through hot coals to feel even more emotional pain, sadness, and despair, I am now going to teach you a process that you can use free of charge for the rest of your life to transform how you feel about yourself or transform any area of your life.

This process was given to me by God, as I described at length in my book *If God Hears Me, I Want an Answer!* Often, people are not exactly sure how to apply this process. So this book is in your hands to teach you how to apply this simple, pure, and astounding process to the area of self-love. The last thing I am going to do is give you a bunch of affirmations that you do not believe, simply because you won't believe them. This is why using affirmations alone will not work. They are wonderful in addition to a pure transformational process, which is exactly what this is: a pure transformational process.

Your Desire for Positive Transformation

If you would like to experience pure, deep, and permanent personal transformation, such as transforming low self-worth into self love, it starts with your deepest heartfelt desire to make the transformation. If you prefer to complain, or you prefer to stay stuck in the feelings you currently have even though those feelings bring sadness, then this is solely within your choice.

Personal transformation requires a deep, heartfelt desire along with an earnest commitment to you. You have to desire to feel self-love, high self-esteem, pure unconditional self-confidence more than you want to remain stuck with the self-degrading feelings you currently have. Moreover, you have to desire to move out of your comfort zone, which means no complaints and no self-insults from this moment forward.

This might surprise you, but the only way you can transform the way you feel about yourself is through your conscious choice. If you would rather put yourself down and continue to complain about how miserable you feel and how miserable your life is, this will do nothing to turn your feelings about yourself around.. So here, right now, it's decision time. What do you really and truly prefer? To feel self-loathing, insecurity, and less than worthy? Or to feel genuine self love, inner confidence, and equal to the rest of the human race no matter whom you are looking at? By forgoing all complaints and self-insults, you will show yourself how committed you truly are deep inside your heart to choose to follow the guidance I am sharing with you step-by-step, guidance that will teach you how to feel self-love.

The process will work only when your heart is committed to it. This book and the processes shared in it will work only when you work them. You could have chosen to read any one of thousands of books, but you picked up this one because deep in your heart you would prefer to actually feel self-love. To feel self-love does require your commitment from deep inside. This is a commitment to yourself, not to me or to anyone else but you.

One Conscious Moment at a Time

It is only in the current now moment when your thoughts about yourself create the feelings you are experiencing. One of the most important aspects of transformation is to become consciously aware of the thoughts you are allowing to continuously go through your mind.

One ground rule for feeling self-love is to stop all negative comments that you make about yourself and the conditions in your life. This is where it starts, and as you can now see, no one other than you can do this. This step will also show you how real self love cannot come from anyone else. If you want to feel it inside, and if you want those feelings to be permanent, un-conditional, then having personal guidelines to keep you on course is crucial. The guidelines are all pure and positive, and will only be helpful to you. I can assure you they work based on following the same guidelines in my own life and working with people from all over the world who experienced pure, authentic transformation. Today, we all feel self love. Now, it's your turn.

Before I teach you this process or the incredibly pure and positive process of receiving answers from God for your own personal transformation, it is imperative that you know how important your conscious awareness is with respect to what goes through your mind about you.

Following the steps in this chapter requires the cooperation of your free will and choice, your thoughts, focus, and paying attention to your gut instincts.

Turning Your Focus Within

As you turn your focus within and pay attention to what you are feeling, you will start to develop self-trust. Giving yourself permission to acknowledge your feelings instead of avoiding them is paramount for self trust, and self love. It is vitally important for you make a heartfelt commitment to yourself from this moment forward to cease all negative self comments to yourself or to anyone else about you. So any of the complaining you have been doing or statements about how horrible you look or how bad your life is or how you don't measure up must be stopped.

The only way to stop the self degrading comments you have been thinking about yourself is to notice when they come up in your mind. Because you have probably been making these negative statements habitually for quite a long time, they will pop back up in your mind for a little while. But take heart, because with this process, they are not going to last. They won't even come up again after a while. Won't that be nice for you?

Conscious Awareness

When an old, negative, conditioned thought comes into your mind, instead of focusing on it or dwelling in it or verbalizing it, simply notice it without judgment.

For example, if you had a thought such as "I'm such a failure" or "I'll never be any good," simply become consciously aware of that thought. Notice that you had that thought, and simply recognize it for what it truly is: an old, negative, conditioned thought—and that's all. It certainly is not the truth about you, that is for sure!

Now, immediately after you notice the negative thought in your mind, tell yourself something positive about yourself, such as that you are a caring person. Or you are an intelligent person. Or you are a kind person. Any positive quality that you truly know you have deep inside will do perfectly fine.

The whole key here is to stop the old, negative cycle because it is vicious, mean, harsh, degrading, and filled with lies about you. Those thoughts came from the level of ego, not from the level of your deepest heart and soul. Once you consciously replace the old, negative, habitual thoughts with statements of truth about yourself, all you will soon be thinking will be truth, and you are going to begin to feel a lot better about yourself as a result.

Speeding Up the Transformational Process

Now I'm going to share a process with you that I shared in my first book, *Individual Power: Reclaiming Your Core, Your Truth, and Your Life*, a process that has helped me tremendously. I have shared this particular exercise with many people, and what it did was speed up the transformation from self-hate to self-truth with respect to what they thought about themselves. After all, if what you thought about yourself was entirely positive, you would, in fact, feel tremendous self-love.

Now I would like to share the ultimate exercise that countless people I have worked with have experienced only positive results when they followed through in action. I wholeheartedly guide you to do the following exercise.

The Ultimate Mirror Dialogue

The exercise I am about to share with you was originally taught to me in 1994 by a wonderful man named Bill Burns. He told me to do this exercise twice a day for two years. I did that, and I noticed a dramatic shift in the way I thought about myself and a peeling away of many of the lies I used to believe about myself.

For example, from age six until well into my thirties, I was called dumb, stupid, dead from the neck up, a nothing, and a nobody. I believed those lies, and this exercise truly helped me to transform them. Although I felt quite uncomfortable doing the mirror dialogue in the beginning, as I am sure you will, too, it is worth doing because it does make a huge difference. And besides that, it is free.

Two times each day, for the next eighteen months to two years, look into your eyes in any mirror and tell yourself three good qualities derived from your observable actions that day. Here's an example. Perhaps you held a door open for someone walking into a store. That action displays the three good qualities of kindness, courtesy, and compassion. Now, let's say you paid a bill, any bill: phone, electricity, food, or rent. Paying the bill displayed your qualities of being responsible, honest, and trustworthy. Here's another one for you. Perhaps you watered a plant inside or outside of where you live. Doing this displayed your inner qualities of caring, love, and generosity of spirit. After all, you could let the plant just die without water, so it does take your inner qualities of caring, generosity of spirit, and love to bring you to water the plant to keep it alive.

Now, when you look into your eyes in front of any mirror, tell yourself what outer action you did and three qualities that you do have within you that were honestly displayed by doing that observable action.

Here's another example of this process. Let's say you do not like the way a situation happened, but you feel good about the way you handled it. This, too, can show you the authentic positive qualities that are within you. For instance, suppose you were in a parking lot and were about to drive into a parking spot when someone else cut you off and snatched the spot from you. Perhaps you thought to yourself, "Anyone who acts that way must not be too happy in his or her life, for whatever reason, so I'll wish the person well and simply find another parking spot." Those thoughts and actions display compassion, understanding, and diplomacy. After all, you could have gotten out of your car and started a fight; instead, you chose to handle the situation in a positive way. Sharing this with yourself in the mirror will help you greatly.

The Ultimate Truth

Here's why this mirror dialogue works. Two times a day you are telling yourself the complete truth that your ego can only believe and not dispute in any way. What Bill taught me and what I am now passing on to you is that if you tell yourself airy-fairy affirmations such as "I love me," your ego is going to laugh in your face along with thoughts like "Ha ha, sure, yeah, right, who do you think you're kidding?" That's what my ego used to do. But when you tell yourself that you held the door open for another person, and that showed honest qualities of being kind, considerate, and compassionate, your ego cannot dispute what you say, because it is observable fact.

Remember that the ego is very much at the five sensory personality level. It is the ego that would say a statement such as "I'll believe it when I see it."

As you grow and evolve, as you begin your process of personal transformation, your views of self are going to change dramatically for the better. As you progress, you will come to say, "I believe it because I see it within my mind."

A Conscious Path

While you are on a conscious path of positive inner transformation, transforming any views of self that are degrading and abusive, after a while you will see that you have come far—and you will feel better. I can share with you right now, just as I did in my book, *Individual Power*, that the very first time I did this mirror dialogue I actually said, "F____ you, bitch. You're responsible, loving, and clean. Bye!" I literally cursed myself out. I definitely did not feel comfortable talking to myself in the mirror. I felt like a lunatic. My ego was not comfortable looking into my eyes or saying something kind, but I kept at it because Bill told me that this process would ally me with myself. And it did do just that.

Bill was also the man who told me that I would be bringing through information from God to uplift the spiritual consciousness of humanity. If you think the mirror dialogue was hard to swallow, when he told me that one, I literally laughed in his face because I thought you had to be a central religious figure like Mother Teresa or the Dalai Lama to receive any communication from God.

As it turned out, when I felt deeply sad, and when I truly did not understand why so many painful things were happening to me in my life, I took out paper and a pen and wrote "Dear God." Then I asked whatever questions were truly weighing on my heart. I wanted to know how to feel self-love, self-value, confidence, and self-esteem. Certainly nobody taught me how to feel pure self-love except for God in the answers I received as the words flowed into my mind that I wrote down verbatim. I must share with you that it took me a long time—two solid years—to believe that I was not insane receiving answers from God in my writings, because I really thought I was. I had never heard of anyone receiving answers from God.

Your True Worth

The core of your goodness and true worth really exists in your heart. This is fact. I know all too well what it feels like to have all kinds of fancy things on the outside and feel deeply insecure and unworthy at the same time.

I also know what it feels like for life to broadside me and strip away my entire reality. I know because I have personally experienced losing it all and being on the brink of suicide. It was because of the countless answers, guidance, support, love, patience, cheerleading, and unshakable faith that God had in me and gave to me in writing after writing that I was able to completely transform my entire life from the inside out. I learned how to transform the way I viewed myself when everything had fallen apart. As God did with me in my writings, I am going to share with you throughout the rest of this book how you, too, can turn around the deceitful, negative, even desolate and sad feelings you have about yourself. Please note that this is not a substitute for medical advice.

It could be possible that if you are deeply depressed, you may have a genuine chemical imbalance; so I urge you to see a qualified medical doctor if you have been feeling chronic depression. You can always receive answers from God. It is important to also take care of your physical well-being. Thinking positively cannot, for example, lower blood sugar in a person who has diabetes and needs insulin. If you need medicine or other treatment from a qualified medical doctor, it is important that you receive it. This book, like all of my spiritual work, is for your spiritual personal transformation. I cannot guide you to heal blindness or any medical condition. If I ever do reach the level of spiritual evolution where I can place my hands over someone who is blind and suddenly they have physical eyesight, I promise I will let everyone know about it.

Back in Time

I want you to think back to a time in your life when you felt good and pure inside. A time when you didn't have any negative views of yourself. If you cannot remember such a time, please find a photo of yourself as a baby. Now, this sweet, precious, innocent, and loving being is you, the real you. Before circumstances got you down and before you were hurt by others and before life got tough, your genuine goodness was within your consciousness, even if you were not aware of it.

When People Put You Down

Perhaps, as happened in my own life, other people put you down and hurt your feelings while you were growing up. Perhaps you were told lies about yourself just as I was told lies about myself. Those people, the same ones you believed or still believe, truly do not love themselves. Anyone with genuine self-love would never degrade another human being. Since you know what it feels like to be void of pure self-love, it is time to simply view whoever told you negative things about you with loving compassion. Why? Because they were in pain deep within and truly did not know how to feel worthy; if they did, they never would have put you down.

The Critics Who Tell You What You "Should" Be Doing

Perhaps there are people in your life who don't truly know how to be supportive of you, accept you unconditionally, and show kindness to you. Perhaps, just as in my life years ago, there are people in your life who seem very adept at telling you what you "should" be doing. Do you know what? They are entitled to their views and opinions, and those views and opinions have absolutely nothing to do with you.

I have traveled this path in my own life. My brother, whom I do love very much, called me "a little left of center." Okay, he's entitled to his views; and I do not have to try to change them or prove anything to him.

Additionally, my mother, whom I also love very much, told me repeatedly to "get a real job" and "work for a corporation" after my first two books were published and I had already worked with many people to help them transform their lives. This was prior to my beloved Mother's recent passing,

Now, this book is about you, not me; but the only way I can help you is by sharing examples from my own life so you know that I have also been there.

Handling Unwanted Advice and Guidance

Now I am going to share with you how to handle the people who perpetually guide you in your life, so you can move forward in the most positive way.

First, stop sharing what you do, your ideas, plans, creative ventures, worries, fears, and business with anyone who is not fully supportive of you. Simply be kind and cordial. When they ask you what's going on, tell them about domestic chores and that you just changed the linens on your bed. When they ask how you are doing, say, "Good! No complaints." After a while, no matter what was happening in my life, when all I discussed was domestic chores and had no complaints, they had nothing to tell me in regard to my life direction because I was no longer feeding them personal information.

The only people I discuss my personal life with are people who love me unconditionally and are emotionally supportive of me. If someone is putting you down, telling you what to do, minding your business, or guiding you, if what they say goes against what feels true to you inside, then simply thank them for their opinion and change the topic of conversation.

You do not need anybody's approval but your own. The people in your life who are quite adept in minding your business most likely are not living their passion, are not filled with self-love, and are not truly working in an area that they would do for free for the rest of their lives if they could. This is where your passion and life purpose come into play, and I will guide you through this as well because it has a lot to do with how you view yourself and how you feel about yourself.

What to Say and When to Say it

If you do not yet have a loving support system of positive people in your life, before you do attract those people, it is imperative that you stick to your truth regarding your personal life and stop discussing it with anyone who is not a positive, life-enhancing support system for you. When people in your life suggest how you "should" live your life, simply say, "Thank you for your opinion." Period. Please realize that many people may think that what they are telling you is in your best interest. Rather than telling you what to do, I am guiding you now to start looking within your heart and asking yourself what truly matters to you, and what you naturally love to do. I will get into this in more detail in the next chapter.

But here I will repeat what I said before: It is so important that you know you are not in this life to win approval from anyone on earth. You are in this life to bring out your real qualities, rather than continuing to tell yourself that you are not yet whole and complete, because you really are. You may not feel it yet, but you will. Your life may look different from how you would prefer it to look, but it will be transformed from the inside out.

Your Talents, Gifts and Purpose

It all begins with getting to know and rediscover the best qualities you have within you, along with all of your natural talents and gifts, so you can align them with a purpose that comes from your heart. That purpose is called your life purpose, otherwise known as the reason you came into this life to begin with, and it all comes from the inside out, not the outside in.

Before I bring you to this place deep within your heart, it is important for you to remember that no matter what anybody says to you or about you, the only thing that matters is that you know the real you, and that you live your truth every moment of your life.

Your Experiences and Worth

The complaints you have about yourself definitely do not reflect your pure inner worth, because this worth resides in your heart. The circumstances in your life, my life, everybody's life on earth are all transient circumstances. This means that they are temporary; not one of them lasts forever. Perhaps just as in my life years ago, the circumstances in your life may be everything other than what you truly desire.

It is important to know that your circumstances never reflect your worth. They are temporary circumstances, period. Your worth cannot be purchased or sold. Your worth has nothing to do with your appearance. Your worth has nothing to do with what you own. Nor does it hinge on a title or a position in society.

No matter what phase of life you are currently experiencing, please know and always remember that your worth is the goodness you were born with in your heart, and from this moment forward, anything that you have been viewing as the basis for your worth can instead be viewed as an experience you would like to have.

Moreover, the critics who may be in your life are actually wonderful catalysts to get you to be true to you. Not to them, to you. Additionally, your truth does not have to be publicly announced. It can remain inside of your heart while you simultaneously move your views of yourself in a more truthful direction consciously, and move your entire life in the direction that reflects the truth you prefer in your deepest heart. It is time that what you feel, think, say, and do all match, in a positive, pure, and life-enhancing manner.

Your age has nothing to do with your worth either. It is just based on a calendar, and I am certain that from this moment forward you have a clean slate in life. You can choose how you view yourself. You can choose what you share and with whom. You can choose who you listen to and who you simply thank for their opinion no matter what they say. Even if a person gives you a negative opinion, thank him or her for the opinion and then remove yourself from this person. Anyone who is going to put you down truly does not belong in your daily life. This applies to adults, not children. Simply stop picking up the phone when the caller is someone who gives you drama, criticism, or harsh words.

Stop associating with people or so-called friends who may be hurtful to you on a personal level. Begin from this moment forward to live out your truth on every level. This truth is that you choose who to talk to and sleep with; you choose the work you do; you choose what you say, what you think, and how you express yourself in your life purpose. None of the above can be chosen by anyone but you.

Now you have a pretty good idea of who is really in charge of your life. It is only you. See the next page if you truly wish to re-create your life and express the reason you came into this life. It is time to know your life purpose.

CHAPTER 2

THE REASON YOU ARE IN THIS LIFE

Have you been wondering why you are in this life and what your true purpose is? What are your greatest qualities? What comes very naturally to you? What do you love doing? What inspires you? Who are some of your role models? I understand that if your life looks and feels like everything other than what you really prefer, it may be difficult for you to come up with the answers to those questions. That's why I am now going to take you on a reverse-process journey that should be quite easy for you.

What don't you like about yourself? What do you despise doing every day? Who in your life is hurtful to you? What do you dread most when you think about where your life is headed? What can you really not stand about yourself? Which people do you view negatively with respect to what they are doing with their lives? You may wonder what those questions have to do with self-love, so I'll tell you. Was it easy for you to know the answers to the above questions regarding everything you don't like? If it was, that's awesome. I care deeply that this book makes the most positive difference in your life. I also need your cooperation because just reading is not going to change your life. True change requires follow through in your actions. Here is what I need from you right now. Please take a few sheets of paper and write down the answers to all of the above questions about everything you do not like about yourself, your life, your work, and the people you view negatively. I can only guide you. I cannot do this process for you. But I did do it in my own life, so I know from personal experience that it works.

Okay, did you write down the answers about everything that displeases you? Please do that now if you can. If you cannot, at least think about those answers. Your life and your view of self are determined by the decisions you make within your mind. Now that you know about everything you can't stand, how would you like it if I could wave a magic wand and make all of those areas turn around? Yes, I know you would like that. But I don't have a magic wand. The magic wand is your own free will and choice, and only you can decide to wave it. If you really and truly desire to finally love yourself, as soon as you are quite clear about what you dislike, you must put those things out of your life.

It is time for you to decide that the people who hurt you are out of your life, permanently. Those things you hate doing? Guess what: as of right now it's quitting time—you get to quit doing those things, forever.

The negative things you think about yourself are what you were led to believe, and you have the mirror process to transform those beliefs, permanently. Remember: to love yourself, you cannot say another degrading thing to or about yourself. You will have to stop giving attention to all of those negative views so that they will stop holding power over you as if they were truth.

Analogies

Now that we brought up what you hate about yourself, and all of those negative views you have about yourself, I am going to share a simple analogy to help you to rid yourself of them, because you were not born with them, anymore than I was born "dumb, stupid, dead from the neck up, a nothing, and a nobody."

You see, I had to work through all of those negative views, so I have created a great shortcut and a couple of examples that can really help you. These analogies will help you with the false views you have about yourself, also known as lies.

Let's say I had a blindfold on that covered my eyesight, and I came over to your house to say hello. Imagine that you were painting a picture of the sky and flowers, and were using colors like blue, yellow, pink, purple, white, green, orange, and turquoise. What do you think your reaction would be if I told you that the brown, black, and grey colors on that painting really did not look good? What would you think? You would most likely think something like this: "Okay, boy, I hope she gets better, because she obviously isn't seeing too clearly, not to mention not seeing at all."

Would you take those comments personally? Would you argue with me to try to prove I was wrong? Would you stop painting? Would you believe me? Of course not! This same reaction also applies to every single false belief you have adopted about yourself.

If your view of yourself is distorted, it is like going to a carnival and looking at yourself in a funny mirror that shows you a reflection of a person eighty feet high and three hundred feet wide. It is not truth. If you have been looking at yourself and the world as a mean, cold, dark, and scary place, naturally you are going to feel scared.

What if I told you that up until now the way in which you have been viewing yourself and your life had a negative filter on it, preventing you from seeing all of the good? This is actually the case, because no matter what the past has been like, it is behind you.

It is no longer your current reality. There may be circumstances that you would like to see transformed, and you most definitely can transform them!

Getting Really Honest

To transform how you feel about yourself, you're going to have to get really honest with yourself. You're going to have to force yourself to discover, live, and express only your truth, so long as it never brings any harm to yourself or anyone else. You know what you do not like, and you can get to know what you prefer by noticing how you feel inside. I know the following is a bit disgusting, but I have to be extremely blunt and go over the top on this one so you can really understand how to know your truth.

Think of your favorite dessert. What is one of your favorite desserts? One of mine is chocolate. If I invited you to come to my house for dinner and I offered you dead bugs for dessert, how would you feel?

Do you notice the nauseated feeling you just felt? *That* is how you know what does *not* feel true for you or right for you or good for you or what you truly prefer. I am positive that just the thought disgusts you, as it does me. Quite frankly, I'd rather starve. I bet you feel the same way, yes? Good. When you feel that way inside, you can translate that feeling into a decision called no, because it is based on what does not feel true for you. Apply that feeling to the list of everything you do not like. Those are the parts of your former life that you now choose to walk away from, leaving them in your past.

Excuses are just that, excuses. I know many, many people who walked away from what was no longer true for them, and they began to thrive as a result.

The people who chose to remain in their comfort zones despite the fact that it wasn't what they really preferred, remained stuck. And nothing changed. This is the difference. Loving yourself comes with the decision to finally listen to yourself. Listen to what your feelings are telling you. Listen to what you prefer.

Whose life is this? Theirs, whoever "they" are, or yours? It is only you who can make these decisions. If you feel afraid, then remind yourself that this fear is a temporary feeling that will definitely pass once you move forward in the direction you prefer based on your truth and your choice to carry out that truth.

Going Forward or Remaining Stuck

Can you swim forward and backward simultaneously? Can you travel north and south at the same time? Of course not. Similarly, you cannot simultaneously live according to your truth and according to the lies or fears that have kept you down.

Everyone feels afraid about moving into new, unfamiliar territory even when it is entirely life enhancing. I certainly did. You are not doing yourself any favor when you continue to hold yourself back from moving in the direction you prefer. If people tell you that you can't, just remember that people told me the same thing. But I did have a grandma named Rose who used to tell me that she believed in me. That meant the world to me, and it still does. I may not know you personally, but I do believe in you because I know that all people who put their hearts and minds into action based on their truth, who focus steadily and consistently in the moment, and who keep moving forward do live a life filled with self-love. This is how I was able to turn my outer life around. It came from an inner decision, one moment at a time, based on what felt true and right for me in that moment, combined with all of the guidance I received from God whenever I felt afraid or unsure about what to do.

I will be sharing the astounding pure process of receiving authentic answers from God, or the name you personally use for the all-knowing, highest source of pure guidance in the universe, with you later in this book. But before you can be true to yourself and follow the process, you have to know what your truth really is concerning every nook and cranny of your life. Then you can transform anything that feels off or not good to you and replace it with what you prefer.

Many of the problems people experience stem from love relationships. I have certainly been through the mill in this area of my life, as I shared in my book, *Stop Being the String Along: A Relationship Guide to Being THE ONE*. Transforming my internal emotional pain was the result of steadfast letter writing to God, asking for answers. That book I just mentioned was all written by God through me while I was going through so much emotional pain. I was determined to turn it around so I could feel joy. This is all I wish for you. Let's take a look at this area of relationships, and then I am going to share many questions and suggestions regarding receiving answers from God so you can continue your process for the rest of your life no matter what comes up.

You are much more than your relationship. It just may be that if you do not feel pure self-love, the state of your relationship with yourself is reflected in your relationship with someone who is or was in your life.

Relationships are one of our greatest teachers. Now it's time to learn some more about them so you can move forward.

CHAPTER 3

YOUR ROMANTIC RELATIONSHIPS

I ask you now to look at the current state of your love life, your romantic love life, and your views and feelings about the relationship you are currently in or—if you currently do not have an intimate romantic partner—how you view relationships in general. I must make one exception for this chapter: if your partner recently died and you are grieving the loss of this person's physical presence, please know that your grief will lessen over time. Meanwhile, you can still glean some insight pertaining to self-love and how you view yourself. Whether or not you are in a relationship now, how do you view romantic relationships? If you are in one now, how do you feel in this relationship? Your feelings about this relationship and your feelings while in this relationship are a direct reflection of your feelings about yourself. If you are tolerating abuse, it is because you believe that no one else could love you. If you are being verbally, mentally, emotionally, or physically abused, the only way you will ever love yourself is to get out of this relationship. I hope with all of my heart, that today—right now—will be the time you decide to get out, because this will be the beginning of your life filled with self-love and joy.

If you feel afraid of being alone and without a partner, this is because no one has yet taught you how to love yourself, to honor your feelings, and to follow what those feelings are telling you, which is why you may feel insecure. You were most likely taught to follow what others told you in order to gain acceptance and love by everyone other than your own self.

How You Feel in Your Relationship

You can be in a relationship and feel completely isolated and alone if this relationship is truly not in your best interest. Finding the courage to remove yourself from a painful relationship comes with your commitment to yourself and with understanding how much you matter; the courage comes with consciously choosing to lift yourself out of misery.

There is no such thing as a perfect relationship, just as there is no such thing as a perfect person. It is the degree of joy or sadness you feel that clearly indicates how you feel about yourself. It is not about the other person or what they are doing. It is about how you feel in this relationship. As I said earlier, getting to the point where you finally love yourself requires complete self-honesty. If you are giving yourself a lot of excuses to remain in a relationship in which you feel miserable, then you are also giving yourself a lot of excuses as to why you do not honor your feelings and live your truth. In short, you are deceiving yourself.

I used to deceive myself, too. I used to tolerate a lot because I had not yet learned how to love myself. Getting honest with yourself is your first step. Admitting your truth to yourself is the only way you will finally open the door to self-love. Of course I will share the rest of this process with you; but there are a lot of bases to cover because there are many different areas of life that reflect how you feel about yourself; I must bring them into your conscious awareness to help you awaken to the real truth inside of you, which is the foundation of self-love.

Perhaps you are not in a relationship, and perhaps you are avoiding one intentionally. I also experienced this phase. I was avoiding a new relationship because I hadn't yet gained enough trust in myself to know that I would be safe by following my truth at all times. Avoidance of relationships is advisable only when you truly need time away from relationships to get to know yourself, who you are, and what you prefer; when you need time to develop confidence in following your truth.

Knowing your preferences regarding your romantic love life also means that if your romantic love life does not match your preferences and if it cannot be worked out to match your truth, then you will survive and be perfectly fine as you graciously exit the relationship. Perhaps you are not ready to settle down with one person. Does this mean that you need to deprive yourself of experiencing joy and closeness, being a true friend, and sharing genuine companionship with someone? Not every relationship requires that you stay in it until your last breath in this lifetime. This is why people get to know each other. Getting to know someone takes time and many experiences.

hen Relationships Change

ou begin to follow what your heart and guts
are telling you rather than any fears or insecurities that
pop up in your mind, you will come to know what
real self-love feels like. It feels like a ride down a river,
a ride in which you are alert, awake, extremely aware,
and going with the flow at each turn. If you discover
that you truly do not desire to share more time with
a person you have been with, then simply move on
with your life. Alternatively, if someone you loved simply stopped seeing you, it is so important for you to
know that this has absolutely nothing to do with your
worth or value as a human being. What if you truly did
not desire to continue to be with someone? Does this
mean that the person is not a valuable and worthy human being? No, all it means is that you have different
preferences.

So if you feel sad over a recent breakup, which is so
common, just know that as you begin to discover and
create joy in your life by moving your life in a pure,
positive, and enjoyable direction, your happiness will
quickly return.

You cannot hinge your happiness on another human being, ever. When you begin to see that you can

create joy in your life by living according to your preferences, you will feel a lot more secure inside. Sometimes people with whom we begin a romantic relationship exit our lives. Any self-denigration that is based on whether or not a person is in your life must be transformed by viewing that person with the same compassion and understanding as if you were the one to exit. I believe you would wish the person well and hope that he or she would be perfectly fine without you.

Now, suppose you meet a new and wonderful person whom you view as a potential partner. As time passes, you get to see what that person is all about. During this time it is crucial that you show the real you, and never put on an act for any reason. As you get to know someone new, notice how you feel when you are with him or her.

Do you feel joy? Do you love his or her company? Do you feel chemistry? Can you talk about anything? Do you feel love? Okay, now suppose you feel this way and the relationship progresses to a point where suddenly you no longer like what you are seeing or how you are being treated. What then? Here's a purely hypothetical example. Let's say I met Mr. Incredible, and we got to know each other, and got very close. Then all of a sudden I started hearing things such as "Honey, it's dinner time." I would not want to go any further with this person unless he understood and agreed that I, personally, do not have a "dinner time" because I eat only when I want to. If he thinks I'm going to conform to some kind of a domestic schedule, he's with the wrong woman. Now, I use this example because this is how I truly feel, and because it easily shows you how a person can have very different preferences that truly do not match your lifestyle. For this reason alone, the person can decide that he or she does not want to continue in a relationship with you. Obviously, this would have nothing to do with your worth. Here's another example. I don't have a bedtime, and I would not want to share a bedroom with a partner. How's that for individuality. I prefer my own bedroom, and if I ever heard "Honey, it's time to come to bed," I would immediately think to myself, "Barbara, it's time to get out of this relationship." As odd as it may sound, this is my personal preference, my truth. And I would not all of a sudden turn myself into what someone else wanted me to be just to please him at the expense of my truth. You also have personal preferences. They may be the exact opposite of mine. Does this make either of us less worthy? No, of course not! So if someone is no longer in your life, perhaps he or she just preferred to live a different lifestyle. When someone leaves a relationship with you, it neither validates nor invalidates your worth.

twisting yourself into shapes and forms just to please someone else. Perhaps you are avoiding love and intimacy altogether. If that's the case, then what you are truly avoiding is both the fear you have of being controlled and emotionally hurt, and the false negative views of yourself that you still carry in your subconscious mind.

Love does not hurt; how we view ourselves is what hurts. If we view ourselves as "out of control" or "too vulnerable and unsafe," then avoidance of intimacy is the symptom. The cause is deeply rooted in false negative views of self. Remember I said earlier that those false negative views are known as lies?

Once you begin to transform how you view yourself, you will completely transform both how you feel about yourself and how you live your life on all levels and in all areas. The process I share with you in the next chapter will bring you truth at a core level, truth that leads to personal transformation, truth that you can receive free of charge, 24/7, for the rest of your life, or until your negative views of self are completely transformed. I will share questions that you can ask God, as you personally understand Him or Her to be, so that you receive the answers that will transform how you view yourself. It was through such questions and answers that I was able to completely transform my own self-loathing views into genuine self-love. This is all I wish for you, and it is my deepest hope that this process is as pure and permanent for you as it has been and still is for me. On the next page you can begin to learn the process of receiving answers from God in your writings so that you can finally love yourself.

CHAPTER 4

RECEIVING THE HIGHER PERSPECTIVE

Many people do not realize that just as self-love exists within, so too do the answers as to how to view yourself with respect to self-love and personal transformation. But those answers, rather than coming solely from the lower self, or ego level, will come to you from your Higher Self, who exists within you and in the highest realm of the universe.

When I did not know how to transform my view of self so that I could feel self-love, I wrote letters to God asking for answers and guidance. The questions

45

below will help you greatly when you are asking for answers, and the process of receiving those answers is actually quite simple.

First, you have to have a deep, heartfelt desire for answers that will help you in your life now. Second, you can write questions that come from your heart. It is important to ask for divine protection, such as asking to have divine white light surround you to protect you. Additionally, if you believe in guardian angels, you can ask them to surround you and protect you as well.

After you have written the question from your deepest heart with a pure desire for an answer, or even for many answers, take at least seven deep breaths so the air goes deep into your belly, and exhale through your mouth. While you are breathing, focus your mind on God, however you personally understand Him or Her to be. While you breathe, you will become more relaxed. If you feel you need to take more deep breaths, this is perfectly fine.

You are simply using your sixth sense, which is always connected to God, your Higher Self, who is the source of your highest and most pure guidance. This is the source of your gut instincts. The source that brings you clarity when you wake up in the morning after going to sleep feeling confused. Please remember that receiving answers from God is not in any way a special ability—it is you birthright to use all of your six senses. This is not a process that you can get wrong; it is a process that has always been available to all of humanity. The only difference between now and yesterday is that now you know that you can use Higher Self communication at any time and for any reason as long as the desire for answers comes from your heart and your motive is pure: to help you with self-love and personal transformation. If others are interested in this process, you can always share it with them from your heart in your own words. But please share it only when people are open to it and ask you about it because people have to truly desire to use all six of their senses. If people are not open to this, then please simply let them be, to grow and evolve at their own rate and in their own way, just as you are.

Suggested Questions for Ultimate Self Love

Here are simple questions you can ask God in your writings. Remember that these are only suggestions to help you with this process. You can always ask anything from your heart.

• Dear God, What has been unconsciously blocking me from feeling pure self-love until now?

• Dear God, Is there a certain thought habit that I can change so that I can transform how I view myself?

• Dear God, Can you please help me learn how to stop comparing myself to others and what the best thing would be for me to do instead?

• Dear God, I feel that I do not matter at all. My life is a complete failure, and I feel like a complete failure. Can you please help me and teach me how to turn this around?

• Dear God, I was told many things about myself that have hurt me deeply. I feel that I don't even know who I am or why I am in this life. Can you please tell me the higher perspective and guide me to transform this feeling?

• Dear God, After I have done a lot of work on myself, why do I still feel a lack of pure self-acceptance?

- Dear God, So many people seem to have it all together. What does it take to be and feel that way? Please guide me.

- Dear God, I feel afraid to do what I really want to do with my life because of what other people may say or how they will view me. Please tell me how to transform this and change it permanently.

- Dear God, I have made many mistakes in my life that I regret, and I don't know how to forgive myself. Can you please tell me how and explain what the difference is between self-forgiveness and self-excuses?

- Dear God, How can I love myself when I look the way I do? I can't stand to even look in the mirror. Can you please tell me how to transform this? Can it really be transformed?

- Dear God, My relationships have been one mistake after another, and I now realize that I have attracted those people into my life to help me grow. Can you please help me become consciously aware of the unconscious beliefs I might still have so I can attract a new and more positive person into my life?

- Dear God, I haven't had the opportunities other people have had to be successful in life. What do I really have to offer? How can I love myself when I can barely pay my bills?

- Dear God, I know you told me to love myself, but I am still struggling with knowing how. Can you please give me step-by-step guidelines, suggestions, and help so I can finally really love myself?

- Dear God, I'm feeling better about myself, but I'm still not happy in my life. I don't like my life. Can you please guide me as to how to recreate my life so I actually enjoy being alive?

- Dear God, My boyfriend [girlfriend] is making fun of me about my writing to you. The writing has been helping me, but I don't know what to say to him [her]. Can you please guide me and give me the perfect words to say so we can get along?

- Dear God, How can I know for sure that it is really you answering me and not what I might have learned along the way? Is there any way you can tell me for sure so I know the answers are actually coming from you?

- Dear God, Sometimes I feel good, and then I get sad again and feel that no one can relate to me. Please help me through this so I can feel joy even if other people cannot relate to me.

- Dear God, My life is changing quickly, and I am not sure what is best for me to do now. Can you please give me the best next steps for me to take so I have pure and solid guidance?

- Dear God, Why in this world would you actually want to answer me?

- Dear God, Life keeps getting harder. I thought it would get easier. Can you please help me to create positive change so I can create more ease and joy in my life?

The above questions can help any person who lives life on earth receive answers from God for authentic and pure self-love and personal transformation.

Fear and Other People's Opinions

I know what it feels like to worry about what other people will think of me. I used to feel tremendous fear and anxiety during that phase of my life when I was facing a choice of either moving forward into the field

51

of broadcast journalism or into the field I am in now and will be in for as long as I live.

Fear of what others will think has prevented many people I have spoken with from following their own truth. Instead, they held themselves back and remained unfulfilled inside.

Nobody can force you to make the positive changes you would like to make in your life. Nobody can make your choices for you. Did you ever stop to consider whether all of the people whose opinions you may be concerned about ever come to you asking for guidance about their lives?

Think about it for a moment. Who are "they" to begin with? Family, friends, neighbors, people who live in your part of the world? And what do "they" think? What if they told you they think the direction you are contemplating is fantastic and wonderful? What then? Would you then have a new worry about success or failure? Would you worry about whether you were good enough in your field of service?

What Matters Most

You see, all of the above—what people think, what you think, success, failure, being good enough—it all comes from the passion you feel about what you are doing, being, creating, and expressing from your heart. That is all that matters.

Suppose you love to teach children. Does this mean that you need to receive the award for most popular teacher every year or a PhD in education to make a true and lasting difference for the children? Don't people and children feel your care? Yes, they do. Don't you feel it when someone truly cares about you? Yes, you do. Do they need a certain title or a certain appearance to touch your heart and brighten your day? No, they don't. What matters most is purity of motive. Moreover, that is what you really feel coming from other people, their motives. If your motive is pure and from your heart, there is no such thing as failure.

Whether a business succeeds or a financial venture profits has nothing to do with the goodness in your heart or with your true worth. No one gave you this goodness and no one can ever take it away. The feelings you have about yourself are completely based on how you view yourself. To transform your self-view to match your ideal, you can come to trust and rely on the process of receiving the higher perspective from God through your writings.

Pure Progress

It does take time and many small experiences to build that trust. As you experience receiving new re- alizations, support, and the pure views you can have about yourself along with how to integrate these pure views, you will come to find that this process is so pure, and so priceless.

It is important for you to realize that your current level of consciousness, those views that you currently hold about yourself truly cannot be transformed at the same level of awareness that you have now. If that were possible, then you would have already transformed your views of self, and you would feel pure self-love and acceptance.

To receive the higher view or perspective, all you need to do is write from your heart and ask your High- er Self to give it to you. Then, reread what you re- ceive.

It is important to reread what you wrote down so you can make out the words, as you will most likely be writing faster than usual and your penmanship will most likely be different than if you were writing with your mind's focus on perfect penmanship.

Understanding, Patience and Support

While you are receiving answers that flow into your mind from God and write them down, you will feel inner peace and you will feel love. You will also feel incredible patience, understanding and support.

You will never feel anything negative, and you will never receive any sort of judgment from God. You will only receive divine, pure, and perfect truth. If you find that you are writing but feel that you are not receiving answers that truly help you, chances are great that you are afraid you won't be able to receive them. You may have views that complicate the process, and you may be asking about the future.

Please realize that this process needs to be done with respect to how you feel now, in the moment, rather than about the future. If your head is telling you that you won't receive answers, then do a writing specifically addressing this doubt. Ask about receiving them if you feel unsure. If you feel blocked, you can always log on to the Higher Self Communication Yahoo Group and post your questions about the process. You will always receive loving support and answers from the group members. This online forum was created to help you with receiving answers from God.

The Level of Your Transformation

The level of personal transformation you will receive through your writings will depend on how determined you are to shed all of your negative feelings about yourself. Your determination must come from your heart because you desire to shed every last lie you have ever bought into about yourself.

Your determination extends far beyond simply reading this book. It must continue after you have read this book and until every negative self-view you have is completely transformed into self-love and self-truth.

The Desire to Receive More Answers

The whole reason why this book was written for you is so that you have a real process to follow for as long as you need to. I have found that sometimes when I received answers, I wanted more. In fact, many times I wanted more.

If you ever feel this way, simply do a writing and ask for much more detail. For example, you might write: "Dear God, please tell me everything I need to know to come into pure self-love and self-acceptance. Please tell me anything I might not be asking about, anything that I need to know that I may not be aware of."

I have written that question more times than I can count. What was so great was that I would receive guidance about other areas of my life that were reflecting negative views I was still holding on to without realizing it. There were still areas of my life that matched the low self-worth I used to feel. This does not pertain to other people; this pertains to how you feel about yourself when you are with other people.

A great guideline that I have adopted and live by is that if I feel negative energy from certain people, I simply wish them well, view them in my mind with loving compassion, and go on my own merry way— away from them. I refuse to engage in ego battles, drama, fights, or anything negative. I learned through my writings that it is my personal responsibility to simply walk away as soon as I feel negativity from a person, place, or circumstance. You have the same responsibility.

The Biggest Lie We Tell Ourselves

There is a saying that I love: "Whether you believe you can or you believe you can't, you're right!" You may or may not believe that you can remove yourself from a negative person or situation in your life. Because this is such an important aspect of many people's life experiences, especially concerning jobs and relationships, I would like to discuss it with respect to moving away from people and situations when you feel anything negative.

If you are miserable in a relationship or a job, and you are consciously telling yourself that you can't leave because of this or that excuse, here's something to consider. What if that person left you? What if you were excused (read fired or laid off) from that job? What then? You would be free of it, and you would then hopefully do many writings to come into your highest and deepest truth about your work life or relationship so that you can create new situations that match your deepest and purest personal preferences.

You have something called choice. When you tell yourself that you can't, what you are doing is putting yourself into mental, emotional, and perhaps even physical bondage. When you ask God, through your writing, for guidance about what to do next, and ask for analogies and highly detailed guidance to transform "can't" to "can"— you will overcome your fears, because this is all the words "I can't" represent: fears.

Fears and Perspective

Whenever I felt afraid of moving in a positive, life-enhancing direction, my thoughts were mainly focused on the future. Moreover, I know of many people who have based their beliefs about what they can and cannot do on their prior experiences that did not turn out as they would have liked.

When you make decisions based on either the past or the future, I can guarantee that they come from the five-sensory ego or personality level. Those decisions do not come from that higher, all-knowing part of you, God, your Higher Self.

If you write about the fears and thoughts, and ask God in your writings to help you transform them into truth to replace the fears, then you will receive the higher perspective. Guess what is going to happen? Your mind and perspective will shift, come into truth, out of fear, and you will truly know and believe that you can choose to do as you most deeply prefer.

Abuse and Personal Responsibility

I know what it feels like to grow up in a home being degraded, abused, bossed around, and feeling the deepest desire to run away. Perhaps you're in a similar situation at home. Or perhaps you used to be. We cannot blame other people for our personal growth and level of self-acceptance. The only thing you can do is decide exactly what your truth is and stick to it. If there is a person in your life who is not honoring you or who is telling you what to do as if you were a puppet on a tight string, the greatest favor you can do for yourself is to remove yourself from the daily barrage of negativity and get into this process of asking God, your Higher Self, for guidance so that you can reclaim yourself and your life.

I have heard many people, mostly women, who were in marriages or live-in relationships, say, "He won't let me," when those women wanted to do something. They allowed another person to literally control their lives, and they obeyed out of conditioned fear.

If this pertains to you, I strongly urge you to do one of the following: Let the person know that you understand where he or she is coming from and that he or she is entitled to his or her views, opinion, and perspective. Then you can say, "I am the only one who can make my choices for me. I am going to do what I prefer because it is my life. I would certainly give you the same personal freedom to do what you prefer to do in your own life. I do not feel comfortable with your trying to run my life for me as if I were a small child. Therefore, please know that you are entitled to your views, but I am entitled to live my own life the way it suits me, for my happiness." Then, do what you want to do!

Alternatively, if the other person tries to hurt you in any manner, including threats, intimidation, or verbal or physical abuse, ask yourself how much you enjoy being treated this way. When you feel your truth, take a brave and bold step into your truth and out of the relationship.

Those are your only two options. I have witnessed far too many people who grew up with a lot of abuse and then attracted abusive partners. I have seen these people suffer, and they are still suffering. I can only view them with compassion. They are people I grew up with, and I can no more tell them what to do any more than I can tell you what to do.

We each have to live with our choices, and when we find ourselves miserable, we have to want to get out of the misery more than we want to remain in it.

If someone is physically abusing you, I would guide you to call 911 and allow the police to remove the abuser from your life. There are laws against physical abuse, but perhaps you live in a country where there are not yet laws against domestic violence.

Many people have chosen to leave situations of domestic violence; they simply started over. The greatest thing I can guide you to do is to write to God and ask for guidance with respect to your own personal circumstance and what you can do now, step by step, one day at a time, so that you can transform a living nightmare into the beautiful life you deserve.

No one has the right to boss you around. But even in America, many people allow themselves to be bossed around. You can receive help if you ask for it. You can start over and recreate your life from scratch. Many loving people are available in this world to guide you toward the help and resources you need on the physical level while you continue your personal growth and transformation on the emotional and spiritual levels.

Transformation and Helping Others Find Hope

You can transform your consciousness by receiving answers from God. You can even write books to help others, just as I do. I never write my books on my own accord, from the personality level. I simply write, "Dear God, Can you please give me the next chapter now in this book so it truly helps people and makes a real difference in their lives? Thank you for divine, pure, and perfect truth in advance. Love, Barbara." Then, I take seven deep breaths, and the words just flow into my mind. While they are flowing into my mind, I write in longhand very quickly, taking dictation. When I say "taking dictation," I mean that I am only writing down the words that flow into my mind from God, exactly as I do in any other writing. Once, when I tried to write a book chapter on my own accord, I was bored out of my mind. It was terrible! I couldn't stand to read it, and I tossed it. That was when I brought through the book *Know Yourself: A Woman's Guide to Wholeness, Radiance, and Supreme Confidence.*

I always do much better when I use all six of my senses rather than "trying" with just five. You can do the same thing, too. You can inspire and help many other people as a result of bringing through a book, a magazine article, or a new business that you actually feel excited to wake up to each day. This process of Higher Self communication is how I and so many other people receive exactly what we need, one moment, one idea, and one decision at a time.

You are no different from me. You are an equal, worthy human being. Your sixth Personal Transformation sense, which is Higher Self communication, receives guidance, answers, direction, and clarification that you could not have come up with previously on your own. Your sixth sense brings you life enhancing guidance, and it is the one part of your nature that nothing and no one can ever take away from you because it is your spiritual nature.

There are wonderful people who may not have eyesight, and they still receive Higher Self communication. They are a beacon in the dark for many people. People who cannot see well enough to read handwriting can speak the words that flow into their minds from God into a recording device and then listen to what they recorded.

Your Desire is Key

There is nothing that you cannot create in your life if you truly desire to. That is the key. It is your desire.

Do you desire to finally love yourself? Since you are reading this book, I would venture to say that the answer is a brilliant yes! Okay, then on the next page you will find suggested guidelines that have worked very well for me, guidelines that I have reconditioned myself to follow. Please know they are not rules, per se; they are suggestions for a list of inner standards to live by, guidelines that reflect self-love. I live by each guideline now, but there was a time many years ago when I did not. During that time, I was extremely unhappy. I had not yet transformed my own negative feelings and beliefs. I hope that the guidelines I share with you in the next chapter will help you have something to refer back to and remember whenever you feel anything less than pure self-love and pure self-acceptance. The guidelines are right on the next page.

CHAPTER 5

EXAMPLES TO REMEMBER

The following guidelines are here for you to refer back to any time you start to feel down about yourself and your life. They will continue to remind you of your active role in your own personal transformation concerning how you view yourself and the self-love that you feel. They are phrased in first person to help you integrate them, as they continue to remind you of your truth at all times and under all circumstances.

1. I am in this life to live according to what feels true for me alone. I listen to myself, my heart,

and I stop allowing myself to be ordered around by others, now.

2. When I am asked to do something that I really do not want to do, I say no. If the person asks me why, I simply say that I do not feel comfortable with it or do not feel up to it.

3. I remove myself from any person or situation that is abusive and hurtful.

4. When someone tries to tell me what I can and cannot do, I thank them for their perspective and let them know in words and actions that I am the only one who can make my decisions for me.

5. Every day I look in the mirror at least two times and tell myself three good qualities about myself based on my observable actions.

6. I remind myself that my worth has nothing to do with my outward circumstances. I know I can change any outer circumstance I feel unhappy about with my decision to change it. If I cannot change the actual circumstance, I know I can always receive the higher perspective about it, which will then transform my feelings to understanding and inner peace.

7. Every time I compare myself to people I admire, I remind myself that I have those same qualities within me, and I get excited about bringing out that part of myself in my life.

8. I do only what I feel comfortable doing with respect to any area of my life.

9. I ask myself what I would most love to express in terms of my life direction and purpose. I get in touch with what inspires me, and then I follow through with my actions.

10. I do writings to God, as I personally understand Him or Her to be, and ask for guidance any time I feel uncertain about any situation in my life, and I ask for guidance so I can move forward in the most positive direction.

11. I remember that there is no such thing as competition. Every person can express his or her own best, and so can I.

12. I express everything in my life from my heart because it brings me joy.

13. I follow my gut feelings and inner knowing at all times, and never allow anyone to steer me away from my truth.

14. I immediately stop all negative comments to and about myself. When a negative thought comes up in my mind, I acknowledge that it is simply an old, conditioned, negative thought, and I replace it with a statement of truth about myself.

15. I stop trying to mold myself into what I think others want me to be, and bring out the courage to be and express who I really am.

16. I share my life's circumstances only with people who are positive and fully supportive of me.

17. I stop discussing my life's problems with people whose shoes I would never want to see myself in.

18. I release all blame on others about my life circumstances, and from this moment forward take personal responsibility to create the life I love to live, one moment at a time.

19. I stop trying to get other people to under-stand me if they do not understand. Instead, I simply allow them their view while I continue

to do what feels true for me, as long as it brings no harm to anyone.

20. I remember that whether or not someone is in my life is never a reflection of me; it is merely a reflection of their preference, and I honor their preference without taking it personally and allowing it to hurt me.

21. I remember that whether I believe I can or I believe I can't, I'm right!

22. I know that what I create in my life is an expression of what fills my heart with joy. It is never a validation of who I am—it is pure expression.

23. I know that outward status does not constitute a person's worth. All people are equally worthy during pleasant times and unpleasant times.

24. I realize that my greatest challenges have been my greatest teachers. I have learned much from the difficulties I have been through, and I help others, even if only by sharing.

25. I create every circumstance in my life, and I do so in cooperation with others, all with pure motives.

26. I use the following guideline to manifest the life I came here to live, beginning with how I view myself:

  A. Decide. I decide how I want to feel, how I prefer to live, and how I prefer to create my life.

  B. Commit. I commit fully to the process.

  C. Be Willing. I am willing to do whatever it takes with dignity and pure motives, including the mirror dialogue, to help me shine from the inside out.

  D. Let Go. I let go of the expectations of others, along with my doubts, and replace them with what feels true for me.

  E. Follow. I follow my truth every moment, and I follow through in my actions everything that represents my highest and deepest truth.

  F. Wait. I have patience with an ever unfolding process in my life, and I remember to enjoy the process rather than just live for an outcome.

  G. Experience. I am experiencing all I first decided to, and now I am living completely in the moment, enjoying this journey called my life.

27. My creative expression is too important to stifle out of fear of what others think. I bring my creative expression out from my heart because I care that it makes a difference while I enjoy the process.

28. My romantic relationship is with a person who is my dearest and best friend. We are fully supportive of each other and trust each other completely.

29. I listen to my body and rest when I feel tired, go for a walk in nature when I need rejuvenation, and consume only what is good for my body.

30. I remember that the goals I am working to achieve constitute every moment of my life, and I live them out with passion.

31. I ask for support when I need it, and allow myself to be real.

32. In my writings to God, I ask to know about anything that is unconsciously holding me back, and how to transform it.

33. In my writings, and each day, I ask to be divinely guided toward only what is for my highest good and the highest good of all.

34. I speak to and treat all others in the same manner that I would want to be treated and spoken to.

35. I stop looking for outward status and start being a pure change that I would love to see in this world.

36. I never explain my personal views or spiritual preferences to people who cannot relate. I share what I choose to share only with people who can be supportive rather than arguing with me to negate my truth.

37. I select my close personal friends very carefully based on the goodness in their hearts, and for no other reason.

38. I remember to ask for pointers and guidance from people who are in a position I would like to move into, and I trust they will be happy to give me a few pointers in a positive direction.

39. I admit my true feelings to myself rather than fighting them and trying to make them go away. They are trying to tell me something I need to acknowledge and know.

40. I create my life's work and purpose based solely on heartfelt inspiration. Passion, not outcomes, fuels my purpose.

41. I fully trust that when something does not work out the way my personality wanted it to, ultimately, it worked out for my highest good.

42. I trust that any delay is a blessing in disguise.

43. I set priorities for my daily activities according to what I feel most inspired to do. My schedule is filled only with what I love.

44. I stop doing anything that no longer brings me joy, with the exception of caring for my children, and clear out any part of my life that I no longer feel excited about.

45. I know that I am the creator today of what my life will look like tomorrow.

46. If I ever worry about what others are going to think, I remind myself that anyone can think many things. What is most important is following through with what I believe in my heart is real and true, so long as it brings harm to no one, including myself.

47. I stay away from drama, gossip, negative people, and negative situations. I surround myself only with people and situations that reflect the pure truth inside my heart.

48. I stop trying to follow what others are doing, and instead create and bring out what I love as my own unique contribution to my life and this world.

49. I remember that no matter how successful a person may be, the truest form of success is a loving and pure heart. That is priceless and eternal.

50. I really can love myself, and I can feel equal to the rest of the human race. I just needed to know how; and now, I do.

Your Actions Reflect Your Truth

The most important aspect of pure self-love is follow-through.

Follow-through means that what you think, feel, say, and do are all congruent. They are all perfectly aligned to match your real truth. For example, if you think you do not like your job, and you feel miserable on the job, then the action that would reflect your truth would be to leave that job. You would then either create your own business or move into the general area of work that fills you with excitement.

When you follow through in that way, you will begin to feel your true worth from the inside out. The same is true for every aspect of your life, including relationships, what you do in any given day, and every decision you make each moment of your life. The key is to follow through in your actions because once you do, you will come to feel pure and genuine confidence. That confidence is built from the inside out, one decision at a time.

I can only share with you that once I started following through on my own truth, and stopped allowing others to guide me in a direction that was completely opposite of how I felt, I finally gained what had eluded me for most of my life: self-love.

I know with absolute certainty that if you choose to follow the guidelines and examples in this book, you will bring out what feels truest for you. As you acknowledge, honor, listen to, and follow through on your truth every second of your life, you will come to feel all of the goodness you really are, and you will ultimately feel real self love.

NOTES

NOTES

About the Author

Barbara Rose, PhD is the bestselling author of seventeen books, a world renowned Life Transformation Specialist, Dynamic Public Speaker, and Leading Global Spiritual Teacher. She is a pioneering force in incorporating Higher Self Communication, the nondenominational study and integration of humanity's God Nature into modern personal growth and spiritual evolution. Dr. Rose is known for providing life changing answers, quick practical coaching and deep spiritual wisdom to people worldwide. She is the founder of International Institute of Higher Self Communication, Global Humanitarian Religious Peace Treaty, and the Foundation for Spiritual Enlightenment. Her renowned spiritual transformational work is highly sought after internationally transforming the lives of millions across the globe. Dr. Rose works in cooperation with some of the greatest spiritual leaders of our time to uplift the spiritual consciousness of humanity.
Her official website is *www.BornToInspire.com*.